The Essential Buyer's Guide

RANGE ROVER
FIRST GENERATION

All models 1970 to 1996

T0373725

Your marque expert:
James Taylor

VELOCE PUBLISHING
THE PUBLISHER OF FINE AUTOMOTIVE BOOKS

www.veloce.co.uk

First published in March 2018 by Veloce Publishing Limited, Veloce House, Parkway Farm Business Park, Middle Farm Way,
Poundbury, Dorchester, Dorset, DT1 3AR, England. Tel +44 (0)1305 260068/Fax 01305 250479/e-mail info@veloce.co.uk/web
www.veloce.co.uk or www.velocebooks.com.
ISBN: 978-1-787112-22-3 UPC: 6-36847-01222-9
Readers with ideas for automotive books, or books on other transport or related hobby subjects, are invited to write to the editorial
director of Veloce Publishing at the above address.
British Library Cataloguing in Publication Data – A catalogue record for this book is available from the British Library.
Typesetting, design and page make-up all by Veloce Publishing Ltd on Apple Mac. Printed and bound in India by Replika Press.

Introduction
– the purpose of this book

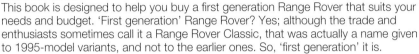

Introduction

This book is designed to help you buy a first generation Range Rover that suits your needs and budget. 'First generation' Range Rover? Yes; although the trade and enthusiasts sometimes call it a Range Rover Classic, that was actually a name given to 1995-model variants, and not to the earlier ones. So, 'first generation' it is.

The Range Rover was designed as a more comfortable Land Rover station wagon/estate car, with car-like performance and driving dynamics as part of the package. And that was how it stayed for its first nine years, until Land Rover Ltd was made into a stand-alone company in 1978. (Land Rover had been a brand name of the old Rover Company, which became part of British Leyland in 1968.)

Land Rover Ltd developed the Range Rover as its flagship model, to meet customer demand and expectations. From the start, buyers had realised that this rapid, practical vehicle was something very special. Its high driving position, superb all-round visibility, smooth petrol V8 engine, towing ability, and everyday usability presented a unique combination of qualities from the start, while its relatively high cost gave it prestige value. But from quite early on, buyers wanted better equipment and a multitude of other improvements to make it a prestigious luxury vehicle.

By the mid-1970s, aftermarket companies were creating luxurious Range Rovers, but these conversions were far too expensive for most buyers. Meanwhile, Range Rovers could also be had as rapid cross-country ambulances, six-wheel airport crash tenders, and police motorway patrol vehicles. This use by the emergency services gave Range Rovers a high profile, and enhanced their image of respectability and dependability.

The original model had only two doors (which Rover's own Sales Department described as 'a tragedy'). The changes began in 1981 with a four-door alternative; and the early 1980s brought better gearboxes (including an automatic) and higher equipment levels. A diesel model arrived in 1986 to improve continental European sales. By mid-decade, the petrol-engined top model Range Rover Vogue had become an expensive and fashionable vehicle, and cheaper imitators were snapping at its heels. Then, from 1988, a Vogue SE model with full luxury equipment took Range Rovers into the luxury-car market, and sold strongly.

The early 1990s saw Land Rover steadily improving luxury levels to keep the model saleable

PBT 946 – the Range Rover that taught me more about the marque than I ever wanted to know ...

until its replacement was ready. Engine power had already been increased, and was increased again; air suspension brought a softer ride; and a long-wheelbase variant delivered a viable limousine for chauffeur use. Although the new Range Rover appeared in autumn 1994, Land Rover kept the old one in production until February 1996 to meet continuing demand for this well-loved vehicle.

Over 315,000 Range Rovers were built (the exact figure is in dispute). Although many have been modified or turned into off-road specials, and many more have decayed beyond hope when repairs became too expensive for their owners, there are still many good examples left to enjoy.

Thanks
I've had four Range Rovers over the years and must express thanks to all the people who helped me to understand them and helped me fix them when they went wrong. One started life as a two-door V8 and left me as a four-door diesel automatic, giving me some unusually comprehensive experience on the way. Thanks, then, to those vehicles, too – wonderful machines, all of them.

... and J180 OAC, my wife's Range Rover which is continuing my education.

Contents

The Essential Buyer's Guide™ currency
At the time of publication a BG unit of currency "●" equals approximately
£1.00/US$1.34/Euro 1.13. Please adjust to suit current exchange rates.

1 Is it the right car for you?
– marriage guidance

Tall and short drivers
Tall drivers have plenty of room, although later models with a sunroof have slightly less headroom than others. Seat adjustment allows short drivers to get comfortable, too.

Comfort was gradually improved over the years; this is the driving compartment of an early 1980s special edition.

The Range Rover was an impressive-looking vehicle from the start, and more so after its mid-1980s revisions.

Controls
Static seatbelts on early models make reaching the heater controls a stretch. Four-speed and early five-speed manual gearboxes feel imprecise with long gear levers. On some models, the heating and ventilating controls can be difficult to master.

Will it fit in the garage?
A Range Rover is 176in (4470mm) long, 70in (1780mm) wide and 70in tall; the long-wheelbase models have a 183in (4648mm) overall length. Standard

Range Rovers also make superb towing vehicles, and this one was pictured in-period with a large caravan.

models will fit into most domestic garages, although you may have to fold in the door mirrors on later models.

Interior space
There is plenty of room for four passengers, or five for short distances unless the fifth is a large person. Rear legroom behind a tall driver may be restricted, but long-wheelbase models give lounging room in the rear.

Luggage capacity
The load area will hold normal amounts of holiday luggage for four people. Late

models with the raised loadspace cover can take suitcases on end, which slightly improves the usable capacity.

Usability

Good acceleration and cruising speeds, plus excellent braking, make a Range Rover a viable everyday classic. But consider the running costs.

Parts availability

You can keep a Range Rover running happily using spare parts from specialists. However, body panels and structural parts can be hard to find. At the time of writing, hopes are pinned on Jaguar Land Rover's plans to make reproduction items available.

Plus points

Range Rovers are excellent towing vehicles and have formidable off-road ability. Most essential maintenance can be done on a DIY basis (less so on the later models). Prices will certainly rise in the longer term, so money spent on keeping one in good condition is unlikely to be wasted.

Minus points

The V8 petrol models are thirsty and therefore costly to run. Build quality was never high, with large and uneven panel gaps a particular problem. A scruffy Range Rover is a scruffy Range Rover, not a valuable classic car.

2 Cost considerations
– affordable, or a money pit?

Servicing intervals

Range Rovers need regular servicing. Typically, they will need a minor service (oil and filter change, check other fluid levels, check condition of brake pads) every 6000 miles (10,000km), and a major service every 12,000 miles (20,000km) or once a year. A 'super service' is needed at 24,000 miles (40,000km). If used in harsh or dusty conditions, a Range Rover will need to be serviced more regularly.

If you use a specialist for this work, the 6000 mile service will cost around ●150 and the 12,000 mile service around ●200, plus, of course, the cost of any additional parts needed, such as new brake pads, spark plugs, etc. The major service will be around ●400. Land Rover franchised dealers will be more expensive than independent specialists.

Sample parts prices

Please note that prices can vary considerably and that the cheapest is not always the best; nor is the most expensive! Many pattern parts are available, but not all are made to OE standards; the prices shown here are typical but you will find quite a wide variation. All prices are shown before VAT is added.

Air spring	●70 (aftermarket)	Radiator	●200 (aftermarket)
Alternator	●115 (100amp type)	Shock	●55 (aftermarket
Brake	●25 (front axle set)	absorber	performance type)
pads	●15 (rear axle set)	Steering	●15
Bumper	●85 (front, bar only)	damper	
	●50 (rear, aftermarket type)	Tyre	●60 upwards, depending
Exhaust	●190 (3.5 V8, mild steel)		on type
system	●340 (3.5 V8, stainless steel)	Wiper	●4
	●250 (diesel, stainless steel)	blade	
	●425 (3.9 V8, sports system)		

Parts that are easy to find

Most mechanical items and consumables – but in some cases you may have to compromise on quality. Some structural items (body sills, lower D-posts, front inner wings) have been remanufactured.

Parts that are hard to find

Body panels, especially bonnets and tailgates. Floorpans are non-existent.

Beware!

Some Range Rovers have been re-engined with non-Land Rover engines, typically diesels. There is nothing intrinsically wrong with this (unless you are a stickler for originality), but do make sure that you are able to find spares for the non-original engine. Ordinary Land Rover specialists are most unlikely to stock them.

3 Living with a Range Rover
– will you get along together?

The most enjoyable aspect of Range Rover ownership is undoubtedly the driving experience. You sit high up, with an excellent view all round, and the bonnet castellations help you to place with accuracy what is really quite a big vehicle. Whether driving fast on a motorway, slowly in traffic, or even more slowly in low-ratio off-road, a Range Rover feels safe and dependable.

There are drawbacks, of course. You cannot throw a Range Rover about like a modern car. Anti-roll bars on the 1991 and later models improved things, but body roll usually inhibits any wish to corner one like a sports car. Although a V8 Range Rover feels quite quick, the figures show that it will be left for dead by most modern small cars. Expect clunks in the driveline on earlier models (there are a lot of joints where slack has to be taken up), and potholed roads will produce plenty of

thumping from the tyres and an uneven (if well controlled) ride. Air suspension on the later models does not make a lot of difference here: these still have big and heavy axles, not independent suspension.

Then there is wind noise. At speeds up to 50mph or so, a Range Rover feels remarkably refined, but at speeds above that noise levels increase. Police motorway patrol officers used to complain that they could not hear each other speak when travelling at speed. A superb double door-seal kit was once available from aftermarket specialists Overfinch, and some experts claim that fitting the softer door seals from a Land Rover Discovery Series II makes

All Range Rovers are very practical vehicles, with ample carrying capacity.

These two pictures show why the four-door Range Rover is a much more family-friendly vehicle than the two-door model.

For maximum rear legroom, the long-wheelbase Vogue LSE is available, but the extra length gives no more room in the front.

a worthwhile difference. On standard models, though, wind noise is likely to be a fact of life – and on those without the chain-driven transfer gearbox, gear whine will be, too.

Strangely enough, a Range Rover that is nearly 50 years old still has what can best be described as 'class.' The name is indelibly associated in the public mind with upper-crust attitudes and wealthy living, so don't be surprised if some of your friends suggest that you're getting above yourself. It will take a long time to explain it to them, so don't bother ... instead, just appreciate the faintly aloof feeling that comes from a driving position far above that of most other cars. You really do look down on the rest of the world – but don't let it go to your head!

Yet a first generation Range Rover is surprisingly invisible to many people. Whereas a classic car from the 1970s will probably turn heads in the street, a Range Rover of similar age will not. One reason is that the basic shape was around for so long, and was so widely imitated that it became part of the street furniture. Outside Britain, you might find that a Range Rover attracts more attention, but at home it is a discreet classic – sometimes refreshingly so.

As for looking after a Range Rover, there are many specialists who can do the job for you competently and affordably. However, don't expect every village garage to be able – or even willing – to carry out the more complex jobs. A Range Rover is not your average everyday saloon car, and specialist knowledge does help. The later your

There has always been something upmarket about a Range Rover...

Off-road ability is superb – but make sure you know what you're doing before you try!

example, the less likely it is that a non-specialist will agree to work on it; there are just too many areas where it is different from the cars that are seen every day.

Do not be afraid to look after your Range Rover yourself. Routine servicing is not difficult, as long as you have a decent workshop manual and the appropriate tools. Buy the parts manual for your model, too (there are several different ones, covering different ages of Range Rover). The ones that Land Rover and its predecessors produced contain exploded diagrams that are very useful for the DIY mechanic. Probably the best compromise is to do as much as possible of the routine maintenance yourself, but to find a local specialist who will be able to help you out when you run into difficulties or take on the more difficult jobs for you.

Finally, never forget that a Range Rover has quite extraordinary off-road ability – far more than most owners will ever appreciate or need. Removing the chin spoiler on late models is a good idea before driving off-road (it will quickly get damaged), and a towbar will typically reduce your departure angle (the angle at which you can drive up a slope without catching the rear of the vehicle on the ground). On models with air suspension, you can even raise the body by a couple of inches before tackling a tricky obstacle. Chunky tyres and two-inch suspension lifts are just not necessary, unless you aim to do some really extreme stuff: a Range Rover is that good.

Early models are much more basic than the later ones. Make sure you don't find the controls heavy.

4 Relative values
– which model for you?

The first generation Range Rover retained the same basic shape throughout nearly 26 years of production. However, there were multiple different models, especially once annual changes became necessary to keep it fresh in the luxury market. So there are Range Rovers and Range Rovers.

Early models were all two-doors. This is one of the first.

The most desirable models, and therefore the most expensive, are the earliest two-door types. They have 'authenticity' on their side, and Land Rover itself would find one for you and rebuild it to as-new condition for £135,000 (or more) at the time of writing. However, the truth is that these are probably the least attractive models of the lot, as they are noisy, basic, and rather less practical than later types.

The least desirable are probably the diesel models, although very late ones can still command good prices. They will all provide much better fuel economy than the petrol types, with up to 30mpg being possible with gentle driving and a manual gearbox. However, most enthusiasts will tell you that the true Range Rover experience depends on that lovely V8 petrol engine, and that means putting up with fuel consumption of between 15mpg and 18mpg – although late models can do slightly better, with care. The brutal truth is that none of the diesel engines had the refinement that the Range Rover really demanded.

Among the four-door models, buyers understandably gravitate towards the later ones with their higher levels of equipment and luxury. Yet early 1980s four-doors also have their own charm, and you should not dismiss one out of hand, especially if it is in very good condition. As for the long-wheelbase models, sellers promote their relative rarity and price them accordingly; buyers, however,

Above left: Original interiors were very spartan, with heat-moulded plastic upholstery, but by the mid-1970s, standard upholstery was cloth (right).

Left: For the first 15 years or so, gear levers were long and the gate felt imprecise.

'Factory' four-doors arrived in late 1981; this is a 1985 Vogue model.

Velour upholstery in a 1987 four-door Vogue, complete with wood door cappings.

With leather upholstery and automatic gearbox, the later Vogue SE models were proper luxury cars.

Left: The four-door Monteverdi conversion was approved by Land Rover before it built its own – but examples are rare today.

The 1995 models had a new dashboard with twin airbags.

The longer rear door gives away that this is a Vogue LSE model from 1995.

should be conscious of the greater difficulty of finding some parts, and of the fact that they offer no advantages to the driver, so make low offers.

Lastly, an automatic Range Rover is far nicer to drive than a manual one, unless it has the early three-speed Chrysler automatic gearbox, which may be bullet-proof, but it is slow and clunky; the later ZF four-speed is vastly superior in every way.

Diesel models broadened the Range Rover's appeal, but lack the refinement of the V8s.

5 Before you view
– be well informed

To avoid a wasted journey, and the disappointment of finding that the Range Rover does not match your expectations, it will help if you're very clear about what questions you want to ask before you pick up the telephone. Some of these points might appear basic but when you're excited about the prospect of buying your dream classic, it's amazing how some of the most obvious things slip the mind ... Also check the current values of the model you are interested in in classic car magazines which give both a price guide and auction results.

Where is the car?
Is it going to be worth travelling to the next county/ state, or even across a border? A locally advertised car, although it may not sound very interesting, can add to your knowledge for very little effort, so make a visit – it might even be in better condition than expected.

Dealer or private sale
Establish early on if the car is being sold by its owner or by a trader. A private owner should have all the history, so don't be afraid to ask detailed questions. A dealer may have more limited knowledge of a car's history, but should have some documentation. A dealer may offer a warranty/guarantee (ask for a printed copy) and finance.

Cost of collection and delivery
A dealer may well be used to quoting for delivery by car transporter. A private owner may agree to meet you halfway, but only agree to this after you have seen the car at the vendor's address to validate the documents. Conversely, you could meet halfway and agree the sale but insist on meeting at the vendor's address for the handover.

View – when and where
It is always preferable to view at the vendor's home or business premises. In the case of a private sale, the car's documentation should tally with the vendor's name and address. Arrange to view only in daylight and avoid a wet day. Most cars look better in poor light or when wet.

Reason for sale
Do make it one of the first questions. Why is the car being sold and how long has it been with the current owner? How many previous owners?

Left-hand drive to right-hand drive and 'specials'
If a steering conversion has been done it can only reduce the value and it may well be that other aspects of the car still reflect the specification for a foreign market. You will not often find this on a Range Rover in the UK.

However, there were many special Range Rover conversions – ambulances, airfield crash tenders, and various other special-use vehicles. These have their own interest but are not everybody's cup of tea. Many ambulances have been converted into campers.

Condition (body/chassis/interior/mechanicals)
Ask for an honest appraisal of the car's condition, and specifically about some of the check items described in Chapter 7.

All original specification
An original equipment car is invariably of higher value than a customised version.

Matching data/legal ownership
Do VIN/chassis, engine numbers and licence plate match the official registration document? Is the owner's name and address recorded in the official registration documents? For those countries that require an annual test of roadworthiness, does the car have a document showing it complies? The MoT certificate in the UK can be verified by the organisations below:

DVSA 0300 123 9000   DVLA 0844 306 9203
HPI 0845 300 8905   RAC 0800 015 6000
AA 0344 209 0754

If a smog/emissions certificate is mandatory, does the car have one? If required, does the car carry a current road fund licence/licence plate tag? Does the vendor own the car outright? Money might be owed to a finance company or bank: the car could even be stolen. Several organisations will supply the data on ownership, based on the car's licence plate number, for a fee. Such companies can often also tell you whether the car has been 'written-off' by an insurance company.

In the UK these organisations can supply vehicle data:
HPI – 01722 422 422   DVLA – 0870 240 0010
AA – 0870 600 0836   RAC – 0870 533 3660
Other countries will have similar organisations.

Unleaded fuel
All petrol-engined models should be able to run on unleaded fuel without modification.

Insurance
Check with your insurer before setting out; your current policy might not cover you.

How you can pay
A cheque will take several days to clear and the seller may prefer a cash buyer. However, a banker's draft is as good as cash, but safer, so contact your own bank for details.

Buying at auction?
If the intention is to buy at auction, see Chapter 10 for further advice.

Professional vehicle check (mechanical examination)
There are often marque/model specialists who will undertake professional examination of a vehicle on your behalf. Owners' clubs will be able to put you in touch with such specialists.

Other organisations that will carry out a general professional check in the UK are:
AA – 0800 056 8040 (motoring organisation with vehicle inspectors)
RAC – 0330 159 0720 (motoring organisation with vehicle inspectors)
Other countries will have similar organisations.

6 Inspection equipment
– these items will really help

This book
Reading glasses (if you need them for close work)
Magnet (not powerful, a fridge magnet is ideal)
Torch
Probe (a small screwdriver works very well)
Overalls
Mirror on a stick
Digital camera
A friend, preferably a knowledgeable enthusiast

Before you rush out of the door, gather together a few items that will help as you work your way around the Range Rover. This book is designed to be your guide at every step, so take it along and use the check boxes to help you assess each area of the car you're interested in. Don't be afraid to let the seller see you using it.

Take your reading glasses if you need them to read documents and make close up inspections.

A magnet will help you check if the car is full of filler, or has fibreglass panels. Use the magnet to sample bodywork areas all around the car, but be careful not to damage the paintwork. Expect to find a little filler here and there, but not whole panels. There's nothing wrong with fibreglass panels, but a purist might want the vehicle to be as original as possible.

A torch with fresh batteries will be useful for peering into the wheelarches and under the vehicle.

A small screwdriver can be used – with care – as a probe, particularly in the wheelarches and on the underside. With this you should be able to check an area of severe corrosion, but be careful – if it's really bad the screwdriver might go right through the metal!

Be prepared to get dirty. Take along a pair of overalls, if you have them. Fixing a mirror at an angle on the end of a stick may seem odd, but you'll probably need it to check the condition of the underside of the vehicle. It will also help you to peer into some of the important crevices. You can also use it, together with the torch, along the underside of the sills and on the floor.

If you have the use of a digital camera, take it along so that later you can study some areas of the car more closely. Take a picture of any part of the car that causes you concern, and seek a friend's opinion.

Ideally, have a friend or knowledgeable enthusiast accompany you: a second opinion is always valuable.

7 Fifteen minute evaluation
– walk away or stay?

There's one more thing you should do before you set off to look at a potential purchase. Having found out from the seller what the vehicle is supposed to be (say, a 1986 four-door V8), make sure you know what specification to expect. You can find this out from some of the books listed on page 56. It is very easy to modify or upgrade a Range Rover by adding non-original wheels, more modern seats, or even a different engine. All these things will detract from the value of a vehicle and may make it valueless to somebody who wants one in original condition. On the other hand, if such modifications don't bother you, but make the vehicle more like what you want, then just go ahead with the inspection.

You can often get a good idea of what to expect from the place where you go to look at the vehicle. Rough area? Farmyard? Back-street dealer? Neat suburban drive? All these things can tell you things about a Range Rover that the seller won't mention. Form your own opinion.

Very slightly down at heel! In fact, this 'barn find' Range Rover was one of the 1970 press launch cars, and has now been restored to as-new condition.

Exterior
The first stage in checking over a potential purchase is to have a good look round the outside of the vehicle. Does it sit square, or lean to one side? Are there scrapes and dents on the panels? What about the paintwork? Is the glass in good condition, or are there chips and cracks in the windscreen? Check the front corners of the bonnet for rust, which is expensive to rectify, and look for the same problem in both halves of the tailgate.

What state are the wheels in? Alloys suffer from kerbing damage and corrosion. What about the tyres? Make sure they are radials of the correct size and speed rating; it is not unknown for sellers to put van tyres on because they are cheaper to buy.

Under the bonnet
The seller may have neglected to mention that the engine has been changed for (typically) a more economical diesel unit from another make of vehicle altogether. If that's

If the tool kit is all present, it's a sign that the vehicle has been well looked after. This is on a 1972 model; arrangements were different on the later models.

How clean and tidy is the engine bay? Few will look this good.

what you want, all well and good. If not, it takes only a second or two to tell whether the engine is of the original type or not; you don't even need to check the engine number because it's easy to tell from the look of the thing.

Assuming it's a proper Range Rover engine, what is the general condition of the engine bay? Remember that the Range Rover is a supremely competent off-road vehicle and may well have been used off-road. Even if it has only been used once in wet and muddy conditions, the likelihood is that mud will have been thrown up into the engine bay and will have stuck there. Not many owners go to the trouble of steam-cleaning the engine, so a muddy (or sandy) engine bay will tell its own story.

An engine bay that is slightly grubby might be described as good and honest: a layer of dust will stick to the oil vapour that inevitably settles on all the components, and not many people bother to clean this off. However, if the whole engine bay seems to be oily, suspect problems such as oil leaks.

Check the level of the oil on the dipstick, and also check what colour that oil is. It will give you an idea of whether the vehicle has been serviced recently or not – and you can compare your impression with what the seller tells you. Check the level of coolant in the header

Corrosion and rust on engine bay components will suggest neglect. This vehicle had been off the road for four years when photographed.

Later engine bays are well filled. A look under components reveals the state of the inner wings – which in this case were severely rusted.

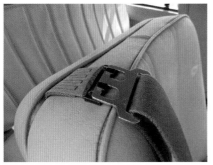
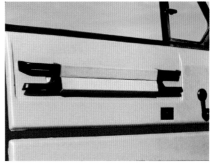

Few early seats look this good – these have been reupholstered using leather instead of the original heat-moulded PVC. Early static seatbelts clipped to the seats when not in use.

Door trims on the original two-door models were intended to look like this, but rarely lasted very long in prime condition.

tank, which will give you a further idea of how well the vehicle has been looked after. A milky appearance to the coolant or a film of oil in the filler neck might point to head gasket trouble.

Have a look at such things as the ignition leads (on a petrol engine). Are they all clipped in their plastic guides, or are they loose and just lying on the engine? What about other wiring, to such things as the washer bottle or (on later models) the level gauge on the header tank? Frayed wiring and corroded terminals mean trouble is lying in wait for later. Then have a look at the condition of the auxiliary belts. Is the fan belt tight? It may be over-tight if it has been specially adjusted in time for your visit.

Start the engine, or ask the seller to do so. Does it start easily, or is there a lot of churning first? Don't worry too much if injected V8s hunt or stumble at first; most do that and then quickly settle down. Is there any smoke from the exhaust on start-up? How does the engine sound as it idles? With the bonnet open, any untoward noises that will be masked during a test drive may become much more apparent.

Underneath

It's easy to check the condition of a Range Rover's underside because of the vehicle's high ground clearance. Just spread a blanket on the ground to protect your clothes and then crawl underneath.

You are looking at two separate things here. One is the condition of the chassis frame and the axles. The

Certainly not an original engine! This is a Ford York six-cylinder diesel, known for its robustness and reliability, but designed for light commercials, and both noisy and slow.

A popular diesel conversion was the Mazda SL35TI, a big four-cylinder that provided good power and torque. This one was professionally installed to a high standard.

other is the condition of the underside of the body. The chassis frame is tough and rugged, but the body suffers terribly, so expect to find some problems. If you don't, either it's an exceptional vehicle or you haven't looked hard enough.

The main chassis frame weaknesses are at the rear of the vehicle. Water, mud and stones get thrown up onto the rear side members, and may well become trapped between the top of the chassis and the underside of the body. Here, they can set up corrosion that may go undetected for years. Have a good feel round on top of the chassis side members, especially above and in the area of the rear axle. Tap the chassis with something like a coin if you are not sure: good metal gives a clear metallic ringing noise, but corroded metal returns a dull thud.

Look carefully for signs of welding. Weld repairs in themselves are not a bad thing – at least somebody has been looking after the vehicle – but cheap repairs are often done by welding sheet metal over a corroded section and then plastering the whole area with thick underseal. It is better to see areas where the original black chassis paint has flaked off than to see the whole chassis caked in a thick compound that prevents you getting a good look at the metal underneath. If there is lots of underseal, have a prod around with a screwdriver to get an idea of what it's covering. If there is plenty of Waxoyl or a similar protective compound, at least one of the vehicle's owners has tried hard to keep it in good order.

As far as the body is concerned, there are three areas to look at here. Most obvious are the splash-plates behind the rear wheels, to which the rear mudflaps are mounted. They are not structural, but they are very vulnerable and do rot through, sometimes leaving the mudflaps with no mounting point. A Range Rover without mudflaps always look strangely naked from behind.

The major area of concern, though, is the body sills. These are essentially rails at the outboard lower edge of the body, and the strength of that body depends on them. So do the outboard body-to-chassis mounting points, and weak or rotten sills are an immediate roadworthiness test failure on structural grounds. On Range Rovers with body kits, the sill cover panels are attached over these rails, and can often make the corrosion worse by making it harder for water and mud to drain away.

You should also look at the body's rear crossmember. Located right at the back of the vehicle, it gets bombarded by whatever the rear wheels can throw up at it, and it suffers accordingly. This crossmember also has the hinge points for the lower tailgate, so any weaknesses tend to be magnified by the additional strain of opening and closing the tailgate.

On the inside

If you're looking at a four-door Range Rover, the first thing to do is to open the rear doors. Look down at the leading faces of the rear wheelarches that are now exposed. They may well be showing signs of rust, and in particular there may be rust around the lower mounting points for the outboard rear seatbelts. Unsurprisingly, that will lead to a roadworthiness test failure.

Now check the condition of the headlining. Range Rover headlinings are notorious for sagging in a less than graceful fashion, as the glue that holds the covering material to the backing pad fails. The backing foam may then disintegrate as well, making repair impossible. The only solution is a replacement headlining – and fortunately high-quality pattern replacements can be had from Nationwide Trim.

Check, too, the condition of the front carpets. Leaks, typically from the windscreen seal, can cause water to sit under these carpets for years, finally causing the steel floor to rot through. It's best to check under the carpets, too. On later models, the sound-deadening felt is so thick that the water may not penetrate through to the carpets, but it will certainly make the footwell go rusty.

The splash plates behind the rear wheels are vulnerable to rust.

Now, what about the condition of the seats? On very early two-door Range Rovers with heat-moulded PVC upholstery, the seat coverings dry out and crack. They cannot be repaired, and many owners cover damaged seats with waterproof or sheepskin seat covers. So lift any covers there may be to check. No-one has yet found a foolproof way of restoring these seats, and you may find that they have been re-upholstered in leather with the original pleating pattern (expensive, and suggests the owner did try) or that they have been replaced altogether with later seats. The Fleet Line models built between 1980 and 1984 also had PVC upholstery but with a larger number of small pleats, and these seats are quite hard-wearing.

The brushed nylon upholstery used in the later 1970s is also quite hard-wearing, but the seat coverings can stretch out of shape and may eventually wear through. Later still, the 'teddy-bear' (velour) trim lasts quite well until its nap wears off. Probably best is the grey velour seen on Vogue models after the mid-1980s, although like-for-like replacement may be expensive if it is damaged. As for the leather option, it is long-lasting if properly treated – which means regular doses of cleaner and hide food – but expensive to replace if allowed to dry out, when it cracks and tears. Even so, leather is probably the easiest of the Range Rover upholstery types to replace to as-new condition.

Door trims on the two-door models were never very impressive, and are often damaged. Clips break and cause the trims to come away from the doors, and water dripping down into the doors can also rot the hardboard backing panels. The trims on four-door models are generally much more robust, although it's wise to check the condition of any wood finishers on the more expensive variants. Replacing the special wood trims on certain special editions will be very expensive, and that's if you can find somebody who is prepared to do it for you.

Special editions

It's beyond the scope of this book to go into the minutiae of the special-edition Range Rovers. You'll need to take an expert along for that, or at least be very certain of what you expect to find before you go to view a vehicle. However, a couple of points are worth bearing in mind. One is that the sort of people who bought special editions often wanted to make them even more exclusive by adding special features of their own; the same happens today with new Range Rovers. This can be very frustrating if what you want is a wholly original example.

Second is that some Land Rover dealers created their own special editions by adding features to make the vehicles more desirable. An example is Gaulds of Glasgow, who turned out Range Rovers with wood and leather interiors some years before Land Rover did it themselves. If you're told that you're looking at one of these, ask for documentary proof that it is what the seller claims it to be. If none is available, be suspicious.

How does it go/sound/feel?

A short test drive will help confirm the overall condition of the vehicle. Expect a certain amount of driveline shunt; even the late top-spec automatics may clunk noticeably when put into gear from neutral. All V8 engines should pull cleanly and smoothly, although there may well be some top-end clatter from worn valve-gear. Diesels are much noisier and much rougher, as all are four-cylinder types. Turbocharger boost may be very noticeable as it cuts in, but there should be no sudden transition; check in the rear window for black smoke when accelerating, which could be either from wear in the injection system or a turbocharger problem.

Does it run in a straight line if you take your hands off the wheel? Only do this very briefly, of course. Does it pull up in a straight line when you brake? Incidentally, on models with ABS, check that the dashboard warning light comes on when you turn the key and then goes out when you reach about 5mph; it is not unknown for an ABS fault to be disguised by removing the bulb from the warning light.

Listen for gears that chatter on the over-run, and make sure that all gears can be selected, including reverse. Select Low ratio (the selector often seizes if unused for long periods) and select the differential lock on vehicles where this can be done manually. On automatics, the changes should be smooth both up and down the gearbox, although the early three-speed box is rougher than the later four-speed. On manuals, check that second and third do not jump out of engagement on the over-run and, on four-speed manuals with an overdrive, check that the overdrive engages and disengages smoothly.

Expect a lot of gear whine from the transfer box, unless it is a chain-driven type. Expect clunks and bangs in the driveline as the drive is taken up, and on the over-run – but the more severe these are, the more wear is present.

Paperwork

Lastly, take a look at the paperwork. Is the seller's name on the documentation? How long has the seller owned it? Problem vehicles are often sold on very quickly.

If the vehicle has been modified significantly, check that these modifications have the approval of the local authorities. In the UK, major modifications may mean that a pre-1973 model is not exempt from road tax in the way that others of its age will be.

Only buy a car from an individual who can prove that they are the person named in the car's registration document (V5C in the UK) and, preferably, at the address shown in the document. Also check that the VIN or chassis number/frame and engine numbers of the car match the numbers in the registration document.

8 Key points
– where to look for problems

Don't take a serious look at any Range Rover without first having a good idea of how it is constructed. Knowing what is steel and what is aluminium alloy, for example, gives you a good idea of what is strong and what is not, what rusts and what simply corrodes into powder. Note that where steel and aluminium alloy meet, an electrolytic reaction between the two metals may cause the alloy to corrode – turn into a white powder.

To those who already know how Range Rovers are built, apologies; I'll be brief here. The vehicle has a very strong box-section chassis and the body is rubber-mounted to this at several points. The body consists of a steel inner skeleton, and all the exterior panels are hung on this; none of them are load-bearing.

The front-mounted engine drives a primary gearbox, and the drive from the back of this goes into a two-speed transfer gearbox. This 'transfers' the drive to both front and rear axles by means of propshafts. Its two ratios are 'high' (for everyday road use) and 'low' (which gives greater control at low speeds for rough-terrain driving). The drive to both axles is permanently engaged, so to avoid axle wind-up there is a centre differential within the transfer box. To give maximum traction for difficult off-road driving, this centre differential can be locked manually – although on post-1988 models a viscous coupling does the job automatically when conditions require it.

The big weaknesses are covered

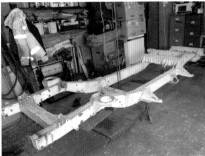

Range Rovers have a rugged ladder-type chassis frame. This one has been painted white to show up its features. On late models the crossmember ahead of the rear axle was tubular rather than rectangular.

This is the Range Rover's inner body frame, made entirely of steel, to which the skin panels are bolted.

Despite its ruggedness, the chassis frame can rust. This one looks bad, but proved salvageable.

in more detail in Chapters 7 and 9, but here's a ready-reference list.

- Rust in the body frame
- Rust in the floorpan
- Chassis damage (and poor repairs)
- Dented panels
- Scruffy or damaged interior
- Smoky or rough engine
- Rough or otherwise worn primary gearbox
- Non-functional low ratio and/or centre differential lock.

This one was not salvageable. The rust had been eating away at the frame unchecked for many years.

The steel body frame can rust badly. This is a rusted-out sill, just below the right-hand front seat.

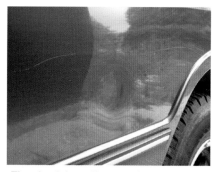

The aluminium alloy panels are prone to small dents, and minor scrapes on the large panels often stand out.

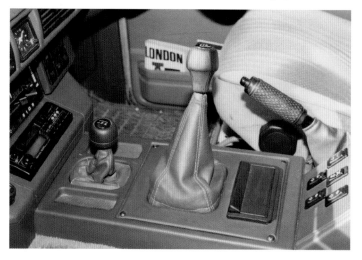

The transfer box control – the smaller lever ahead of the gearlever here – can sometimes seize through lack of use.

9 Serious evaluation
– 60 minutes for years of enjoyment

Score each section using the boxes as follows:
4 = Excellent; 3 = Good; 2 = Average; 1 = Poor
The totting-up procedure is explained at the end of the Chapter. Be realistic in your marking!

The best way to use this section is to tick the boxes as you go along, because you won't be able to remember all the details of the vehicle when you sit down to think about it later on. The inspection sequence follows a logical order, so you'll start with the outside of the vehicle, move on to the interior, then examine the engine bay and the underside. If you're doing your inspection at a dealership or a specialist's premises, ask if you can put the vehicle on their hoist or ramp to make the underside inspection easier. Last of all, you'll take a test drive.

Paintwork

As always, you have to score this section relative to your needs. If you are looking for perfect original condition, then a respray in a non-original colour, however good it may be, will not rate highly. On the other hand, if you just want something you can run around in while you tidy it up, your standards won't be as high.

The standard factory paint finishes varied enormously. Early 'solid' colours were applied in a workmanlike fashion, and spraying a new panel to match is not difficult. Things became more difficult with the later metallics and micatallics, where repainting a damaged area or spraying a new panel will often cause difficulties with matching. The later paints have a clear lacquer top coat, and this can sometimes peel off in small areas. Unfortunately, the only remedy is to strip the panel right back and paint it again. The very best finishes are seen on colours such as Beluga Black (1989-1996 model-years), but these also look the worst when neglected.

It's probably best to score this section according to how much work you think you'll want to do on the paint: a low score means you'll want to do a lot, a high score means virtually none.

Body panels

It's important to remember that the wings and door panels are made of aluminium alloy. They will be more prone to minor dents and creases than steel panels, but will not rust. Instead, you may find a

Check metallic and micatallic paints carefully for areas like this, where the clear top coat has peeled away.

Check for aluminium corrosion where alloy panels meet the steel body frame. The tops of the front wings are a favourite spot.

crumbly white powder in the areas where aluminium and steel meet. This is the electrolytic corrosion mentioned in Chapter 8.

Shut lines

Land Rover never did get the shut lines as narrow or as consistent as luxury-car customers expected. Part of the problem was the tolerances built into the original bolt-together body frame, and part of it was an unwillingness to invest in new tooling. So don't be disappointed to find large gaps between panels. Even specially-prepared press vehicles had them, although they were minimised as much as possible. You might find minor panel misalignment, as well, not least around the scuttle.

The poor fit of the scuttle panel is apparent on this vehicle, which was actually a 1994-model LSE press demonstrator!

Front wings/fenders

There are several varieties of front wing, early ones with cut-outs for the door hinges and late ones without. There have also been different positions for the indicator repeater lamp, so don't be surprised to find that the original hole has been filled in or that the lamp is in the wrong place!

Collision damage apart, the main threat to front wing panels is from electrolytic corrosion, where they bolt to the tops of the steel inner wings. Reproduction front wings in GRP were available many years ago, and may turn up on early two-door models, and more recent reproduction panels have been made of ABS plastic. Gently rapping on the panel with your fingers will give you a good idea of whether it's metal or not; so will feeling the turned-under edges of the wheelarch.

Bonnet

The bonnet panel is big and heavy, and on later models has a torsion bar spring to make it easier to lift. There have been two basic types, with and without exposed hinges, and they are not interchangeable. Bonnet panels of all ages suffer from rust in the front corners, and this can be tricky to repair. However, as there have been no new bonnet panels for some time, it is becoming more and more likely that rusty bonnets will have to be repaired. Check also for rust in the bonnet

The whole bonnet is steel, with an outer skin mounted on a frame. The frame can rust: rusted areas are seen here painted with a rust-retardant primer.

The front corners of the bonnet can rust out.

frame, usually caused by long-term neglect of cleaning under the bonnet when mud and water have accumulated after an off-road driving session.

Doors

The doors have aluminium alloy skins over steel frames, which gives ample opportunity for corrosion to break out where the two metals meet. The outer skins will probably have a few minor dents, and only you know whether you can live with these or will want to have them rectified. Rectification typically involves the use of filler and then a full panel respray; the alloy hardens when worked, and so beating out the dent is often not viable.

The big doors on two-door models are very heavy, so check the front face of the door frame for its soundness around the hinge fixing points. All doors have drain holes in their bottom faces, but these holes can become blocked over time. Water running down the windows and past the seals into the door cavities will then be trapped against the inside of the frame which will, inevitably, rust out. Repairing a door frame is a time-consuming job; in some cases, it may be impossible.

Small areas of aluminium corrosion like this one, at the top of a rear door, are easy to miss unless you look carefully.

Roof panel & sunroof (if fitted)

Check for dents and dings in the big roof panel, often caused when a roof rack has been fitted or removed. A few early vehicles will have been fitted with Webasto or similar sliding fabric sunroofs, but these are not common – and they tend to add to the noise level at speed. If the edges have begun to curl up as the fabric shrinks, budget for a complete replacement, which won't be cheap.

Land Rover made an electrically-operated slide-and-tilt sunroof panel available from 1988. Check that it works properly. Early examples have a metal sliding panel but later examples have a glass panel. With the glass panel, there is a separate interior screen panel that is operated by hand: check that it slides properly and that the fabric lining (which should match the headlining) is correctly secured to it.

Note that the factory-installed sunroof is actually a self-contained cassette unit that bolts under the roof panel. It does reduce headroom in the front slightly.

Sills/rockers, side-steps

The visible sill panels are made of black plastic, unless somebody has bolted rock sliders or some similar heavy-duty protection to the vehicle. The early sills are quite slim and are bolted to the body frame. They can crack under impact, especially along a mould line towards the rear. The later sills (from summer 1989) are much deeper, to help hide the Range Rover's underpinnings, and are shared with the contemporary Discovery models.

From 1992, a bodykit was available as a factory accessory, and this was attached by brackets screwed to the body frame (and often by cable-ties as well!). Those brackets can rust through, and the screw-holes may cause the metal body frame to rust.

Some vehicles will have been fitted with side-steps, either using the factory accessory or an aftermarket equivalent. If these steps are bent or otherwise damaged, replacing just one will be a problem, so budget for replacing two – or leaving them off altogether.

The lower D-posts

The D-posts on four-doors can rust at their joins with the sills (as here), and also around the seatbelt mounting points.

You will have formed an initial impression of the lower D-posts on a four-door Range Rover during your 15-minute evaluation. These will be black on earlier models but body-coloured on 1991 and later models. Look for rust at the bottom where they meet the sills of the body frame, rust around the welds where the curved sections meet the vertical pillars and, of course, rust around the mountings for the seatbelts. Fortunately, complete replacement lower D-posts are available, but welding them in properly requires a degree of skill.

Rear wings/fenders

There are no special concerns with the rear wings, although check that they have not been distorted at the bottom by contact with rocks and the like when the vehicle has been driven off-road. The fuel filler is on the right rear wing on all models. Early ones have a dished plate let into the wing around the filler. From the mid-1980s the filler was concealed by a hinged door made of plastic, which locked when the central locking was activated. From 1991, the filler was mounted higher up the wing, again with a plastic fuel filler door. In this case, the door was released electrically by a button on the steering column. Beware of filler doors that have been forced open or will not close properly.

Upper tailgate

Despite the protective coverings, top tailgates rust at their lower corner seams.

The upper tailgate is notorious for rusting, which begins in the lower corners where the vertical parts of the steel frame meet the lower rail at a 45-degree angle. After the mid-1980s, these rust-prone joins were concealed under plastic cover plates, which may well have retarded the rusting but certainly did not prevent it. The lower edge of the rail, concealed behind a rubber seal, also rusts badly.

New tailgates have been virtually unobtainable for some time, although aftermarket replicas with aluminium frames have been available. These are sometimes prone to a degree of twisting if they are not treated properly; the best way to close one (and a good way of closing a factory-made tailgate with steel frame) is to apply equal pressure to both sides of the bottom rail.

Worth knowing is that there were several different types of tailgate glass, and that there are types with or without a tint to match the rest of the vehicle's glass. The earliest models always had an unheated glass panel. There was then a heated glass panel with elements which did not reach all the way to the bottom of the tailgate. In the later 1970s came full-depth elements that ran straight from side to side, and finally there was a tailgate glass with U-shaped elements that doubled as antenna for the radio. After 1990, the top tailgate for some export territories incorporated a third brakelight just above the handle; this was known as a CHMSL (centre, high-mounted stop light).

Lower tailgate

4️⃣ 3️⃣ 2️⃣ 1️⃣

As with the upper tailgate, so with the lower section: it rusts. Look particularly in the underside at the bottom, at the seams around the 'step' in the panel, and at the sides. Repairs are not always viable, and new tailgates are simply not available. There were several varieties of lower tailgate, too,

Rust in the lower tailgate is also very common.

early ones with an external release handle and late ones with an internal handle. You might have to wait a while to find the correct type secondhand.

Loadspace floor

4️⃣ 3️⃣ 2️⃣ 1️⃣

The ribbed loadspace floor may be concealed under a rubber mat on early models, or it may be concealed under carpet and sound-proofing on later Range Rovers. Or it might just be hidden under a pile of old sacking and carpet off-cuts; it depends how the owner has treated the vehicle.

Whatever the case, you need to get a good look at it because the early aluminium alloy type of floor panel corrodes, and the later steel type rots badly. Lifting the

The rear load floor may be hidden under the carpet. Look out for rust underneath.

A load floor replacement created by welding an extension section to a Discovery floor panel.

carpet is not a quick operation, so tell the seller what you plan to do and allow time to put everything back properly. If the floor is corroded or rotten, budget for a complete replacement. At the time of writing, no panels were available, and the solution was to use a Discovery floor panel with an extension piece welded to it.

Windscreen frame

4️⃣ 3️⃣ 2️⃣ 1️⃣

All models built before the 1995 model-year had conventional rubber-glazed windscreens, and the final ('soft-dash') models had bonded windscreens. The rubber glazing can perish or become damaged and let water through. Similar water ingress can occur with the bonded screens, typically if the original screen has been replaced and the bonding was not conscientiously applied all the way round the screen.

The bottom of the spare wheel recess can also rust out.

The water does not always make its way through to the inside, where it is likely

The windscreen aperture is vulnerable to rust; here, a leak had caused the lip holding the glass to rot out.

to stain the headlining. It may only go as far as the lip on the windscreen frame, which will then rust through. You won't discover how bad this is until the next time you come to change the windscreen, but repairing it will require considerable skill.

Bulkhead and footwells

④ ③ ② ①

The bulkhead is not the easiest part of a Range Rover to examine, but you should be aware that it can rot out. Typically, the side panels of the footwells will rust through; less commonly, blocked drain holes will lead to rust in the top section as well.

If the problem is only in the footwells, you can weld in patch panels supplied by the specialists. If the rot is more extensive, you may have to replace the whole bulkhead. That is a major job, which involves taking the body off the chassis. On early models with bolt-together body frames, replacement with a sound bulkhead from a contemporary model is viable, as

Typical rust damage to the front footwell and bulkhead area is seen here on a 1989 Range Rover. The only remedy on these later shells, where the bulkhead is welded to the frame, is careful patching.

long as you can find a donor vehicle. However, the job is much more tricky on the later models with all-welded body frames, because the bulkhead is an integral part of that frame.

To summarise, then, major bulkhead damage comes into the major cost category. Steer clear unless you are prepared for that.

The engine bay

④ ③ ② ①

If a non-original engine is fitted, you will have spotted that in your earlier 15-minute evaluation. However, if you have decided to proceed this far with a detailed evaluation, you now need to find out more about the engine. There were several reputable companies in the 1980s that provided excellent diesel engine transplants, to suit customers who wanted better fuel economy. There were also several DIY conversions, and not a few rapid bodges, so it is important to find out who did the conversion, and when.

Equally important is to find out whether you can still get parts for it today, and what special components (often sourced from other vehicles) might have been used. A favourite was to use radiator hoses that were readily available at the time but might not be so easily available now – especially if you don't know what vehicle they come from! An expert parts man at your local motor factor might be able to identify where a top hose came from – or he might not.

In that connection, it is worth knowing that, from the early 1990s, Land Rover offered a kit to fit its own Tdi diesel engine into Range Rovers. There were versions to suit both 200Tdi and 300Tdi engines, and to suit both V8 and VM diesel host vehicles. Many kits were installed by Land Rover dealers, and in general these can be considered to have been done to factory standards.

You should be relatively free from concerns of this sort if the vehicle still has its original (or original type) engine. Assuming the basic checks you did in your 15-minute evaluation left you reassured that the seller has not neglected its maintenance, the next thing is to listen to the engine running.

The diesels are noisy, although the indirect-injection VM types and the 300Tdi are generally quieter than the 200Tdi. You are unlikely to hear any untoward noises above the general din, so suspend your disbelief until you road-test the vehicle. The petrol V8s are quieter and smoother, but they can also suffer from a variety of strange noises, most of which do not indicate anything serious. Again, wait until you road-test the vehicle, when any serious problems will become apparent.

Checking under the car

You can see most, but not all, of what you need to see under a Range Rover fairly easily, because of the vehicle's high ground clearance. Just spread out a blanket or similar on the ground under the vehicle, and get under there to take a look. That said, it is much more comfortable to do the job if the vehicle can be raised on a hoist first, so if the seller has one (and most garages do), ask if you can use it.

Oil leaks 　　　　4️⃣ 3️⃣ 2️⃣ 1️⃣

If the vehicle is suffering from oil leaks, the evidence will be immediately visible when you get underneath. If you can, check where the oil is coming from; worn-out sealing washers on sump plugs and axle drain plugs are often the culprit. Cracked casings that are leaking should be very obvious.

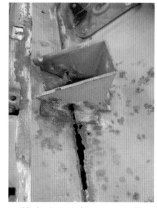

Unfortunately, you won't be able to see this: it's rust underneath the scuttle panel, below the windscreen.

The bulkhead on early Range Rovers is bolted to the body frame. This is a secondhand replacement being painted, ready for fitting.

This kind of chassis rust can go unnoticed for a very long time because it is hidden between chassis and body.

Of course, you will then have to assess whether the seller has tried to keep oil levels up to their correct levels despite the leaks, or has simply trusted to luck.

Chassis frame

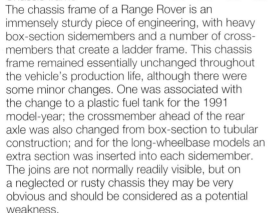

The chassis frame of a Range Rover is an immensely sturdy piece of engineering, with heavy box-section sidemembers and a number of cross-members that create a ladder frame. This chassis frame remained essentially unchanged throughout the vehicle's production life, although there were some minor changes. One was associated with the change to a plastic fuel tank for the 1991 model-year; the crossmember ahead of the rear axle was also changed from box-section to tubular construction; and for the long-wheelbase models an extra section was inserted into each sidemember. The joins are not normally readily visible, but on a neglected or rusty chassis they may be very obvious and should be considered as a potential weakness.

The long-wheelbase chassis was created by welding an extra section into the sidemembers. Despite the high quality of construction, the joins will eventually begin to rust.

Serious rust on the chassis is not a particularly big problem on a Range Rover, although there may well be plenty of surface rust. The sidemembers contain drain holes that can become blocked, and if they are blocked they have probably trapped water inside. Eventually, this will cause the frame member to rust from the inside out, so keep a look out for clusters of rust-coloured pin-holes, especially in the lower corners of the box-sections. Take a very careful look at any patches that have been welded to the chassis, because only in very high quality repair work will the metal underneath have been cleaned up and de-rusted first. A welded patch means there has been a problem, and the chances are that the problem will re-appear in due course.

Anti-roll bars were a very welcome addition; this one is on the rear axle. With Land Rover's own kit, the U-shaped brackets were bolted into the chassis sidemembers; if fitted on assembly, they were welded.

However, there is one area where you should always check very carefully, and that is above the rear axle, and sometimes behind it as well. Debris thrown up by the rear wheels can have the effect of shot-blasting the paint off the sidemembers, and when unprotected they are likely to start rusting. More insidious, however, is rust on the top of the chassis frame, where it cannot be seen. Road debris can accumulate between the sidemembers and the underside of the body, and eventually the top surface of the frame can rust through. Check for this by feeling in the gap with your fingers. If the frame is rusty here, there is no quick remedy. The body will have to come off, and you may end up replacing the entire chassis once you have assessed the extent of the damage. It goes without saying that this is a massively time-consuming and potentially expensive job.

Check that all four axle bump-stops are present; these are the rubber buffers above the axle on each side, that prevent the axle casing from coming into contact with the chassis frame over extreme bumps. They are easy enough to replace, but it's sensible to check the area where they are mounted in case it is already suffering from impact damage or rust.

The bump-stops are mounted to the chassis on metal carriers. In this case, the bump stop had fallen off and the carrier had rusted through as well.

All Range Rovers that have been used off-road with any degree of seriousness are likely to bear the scars of the experience on their chassis frames. Typically, the frame may strike a rock or other large solid object, which will leave a dent. Unless those dents are showing signs of rusting, do not worry about them – although you can of course use them as a bargaining counter when trying to strike a deal with the seller.

Fuel tank

All Range Rovers had a steel fuel tank at the rear of the chassis until January 1991, when a plastic tank became standard. The plastic tank has multiple advantages, but the two types of tank are not interchangeable. The chassis mountings differ between them, and the plastic tank has a longer filler neck.

Check both types of tank for the security of their fixings and any signs of impact damage. Check the steel tank for signs of corrosion, which may result from water in the fuel, or condensation in an empty tank that has started rusting from the inside. Tanks may leak around their seams if they have been subject to unusual stresses, and you can detect leaks easily enough by their smell, especially on petrol models.

Various types of auxiliary fuel tank have been available from aftermarket specialists to increase the fuel capacity and therefore the range between fill-ups. There have also been special tanks for Range Rovers converted to run on LPG, which was a popular way of reducing fuel costs in the 1990s, even if the payback time for the installation of the system was quite lengthy. If an LPG system has been fitted, ask to see evidence that the system has been checked and approved as safe by an appropriate authority.

Front suspension towers

The front suspension towers are the large cone-like structures that are bolted to the chassis above the front axle, and act as anchors for the top mountings of the dampers. Although you can certainly see the problem areas from underneath, it is probably advisable to take a second look from above when the bonnet is open.

The towers are likely to rust around their fixing flanges at the bottom, where they are mounted to the chassis. Weak flanges are potentially dangerous because a severe shock load through the spring could cause the suspension tower to come adrift. This is most likely to occur during heavy-duty off-road driving, but you can just imagine the consequences if it were to happen during fast road driving.

Look for rust around the base of the front suspension towers, where they bolt to the chassis.

The Hydromat self-levelling strut on the rear axle should not be leaking.

The axle casings may also show signs of off-road damage, typically around the differential housings, because these hang lower than the rest of the casing. Severe damage is likely to lead to leaks from the differential, although these will be easy enough to spot.

The Range Rover's long-travel coil-spring suspension allowed some quite fearsome body roll in cornering, but it wasn't until 1990 that the company made a kit of anti-roll bars – one on each axle – available. These were later standardised. There was also an anti-roll bar kit that could be retro-fitted to earlier Range Rovers, and of course there were aftermarket kits as well from quite early on. Worn rubber bushes will cause the anti-roll bars to lose their effectiveness, but there can be a bigger problem with their mountings. These are welded to the chassis on the factory installation, but the factory kit depended on attaching them to the chassis with Riv-nuts that fitted into holes drilled in the undersides of the sidemembers for the purpose. In some cases, if the chassis members have since deteriorated, the Riv-nuts may pull right out, leaving the anti-roll bars ineffective.

At each end of the front axle is a chromed ball, which swivels to allow the wheels to be steered. The chromed faces that you can see should be smooth and not pitted or rusted. If sand or mud becomes trapped under the swivel seals, it will eventually scratch or erode the chrome surface so that the seal cannot work effectively, and at this point oil begins to leak out. Oil is essential to the workings of the steering here, and severe oil leaks indicate that the ball swivels (and maybe more) will need to be replaced.

On the rear axle, check the security of the brake pipes that run along its casing. They will probably be held in place by plastic ties, but that is quite good enough to keep them out of harm's way.

Just ahead of the rear axle is a large A-frame, which helps to locate it centrally. The frame itself is unlikely to be a source of trouble, but you should check the condition of the self-levelling strut that is mounted within it. Called a Boge Hydromat, its function is to prevent heavy loads in the rear of the vehicle from causing it to drag its tail, to the detriment of the handling. As the vehicle moves, so the strut automatically pumps itself up to give the correct ride height. It can of course leak oil, when it will equally obviously not function properly. The strut can be replaced easily but is not cheap. Note that Range Rovers with air suspension still have the A-frame, but do not have the Boge strut: the air suspension system carries out the self-levelling function automatically.

Suspension springs: steel or air

Long-travel coil springs were essential to the Range Rover's original design, and they proved sturdy and reliable. It is not impossible to break one, but any such damage will be readily visible and should be a warning that the vehicle has probably suffered some serious abuse. On vehicles which have had a suspension lift, make

On air-sprung models, the black rubber 'spring' fits between axle and chassis, in place of the steel coil spring. This is it in place on the rear axle.

sure that the job has been done properly because changing the distance between chassis frame and axle casings requires more alterations than many people seem to think.

From mid-1992, top model Range Rovers came with air suspension instead of steel coil springs. There is a compressor mounted on the right-hand chassis rail, a valve block on the other side, and a sophisticated electronic control system. The air suspension reduces the amount of noise transmitted into the vehicle body by de-coupling the axles from the rest of the structure. It also allows a degree of height control, so the vehicle can be lowered to aid passenger entry, it will lower itself automatically to improve handling at speed, and can be raised to help clear off-road obstacles.

The air springs occasionally need to be replaced when they develop a leak. Typically, this is caused by the rubber 'bag' fretting against its steel mounting on the axle casing, so look for signs of wear here, and ask when the air springs were last replaced. A severe air leak will cause the compressor to run continuously as the system tries to provide enough air to fill the leaking spring, and eventually the compressor will burn out. Compressors are expensive; air springs are not – and can even be replaced on a DIY basis. So check carefully here to avoid big bills later.

Brakes

All Range Rovers have disc brakes on all four wheels, which give superb stopping power when in good order. Beginning with the 1990 model-year, the front discs were ventilated to give an extra margin of safety. Check that the correct discs are fitted and that they are in good order. It would be unwise to fit solid discs in place of the ventilated type, although the temptation is there because they are cheaper. Aftermarket cross-drilled discs have been made available, and seem to do a good job as replacements.

Ideally, brake discs should be smooth and unmarked, like this one which was pictured when new on a 1990 model. It is a ventilated front disc.

The handbrake operates on a drum directly behind the transfer gearbox. It locks movement of the rear propshaft, but of course cannot

The reality is sometimes shocking: this ventilated disc had corroded badly and had cracked across the vents.

35

compensate for any movement in the propshaft's universal joints. It is this which accounts for the slight lurch that often occurs on a slope before the handbrake engages – a feature which many people find worrying. It is not unknown for the transmission brake itself to be damaged by a severe impact in off-road driving, but this sort of damage will be immediately apparent.

Check around the filler plugs and drain plugs for signs of oil leaks, and examine the exhaust for signs of corrosion as well.

Steering ④ ③ ② ①

Power-assisted steering became optional on Range Rovers quite early on, and subsequently became standard, so most examples you will look at are going to have it. Major fluid leaks, from either the hydraulic pipes or from the steering box, will prompt refusal of a roadworthiness certificate. The suspension may groan and creak if the wheels are turned on a hard surface while the vehicle is stationary (as often happens in parking manoeuvres). However, hissing noises from the hydraulic system suggest a problem.

To test for steering problems, you need to have an assistant. Ask the assistant to turn the steering wheel from side to side while you lie under the vehicle and check for movement in the steering linkages. There are problems if you can see any movement at all between the swivel pin housing and the swivel steering lever at the point where they are bolted together. Free movement in any of the steering assembly's ball joints points to wear, and – obviously – fluid leaks or oil leaks that become apparent during this test are a sign of problems.

Shock absorbers ④ ③ ② ①

Early Range Rovers have 'staggered' shock absorbers at the rear; the left-hand damper is attached to the chassis ahead of the axle, and the right-hand one is attached behind the axle. This was changed on the 1986 models, so that both dampers were mounted to the chassis ahead of the axle.

It is difficult to test the shock absorbers on a Range Rover by the sort of bounce test that people commonly use for cars. It is also unwise: you might dent a panel.

Propshafts ④ ③ ② ①

You should always check for wear in the transmission by grasping the front and rear propshafts in turn, and trying to twist them manually. They will turn slightly as slack in the system is taken up, but if either will rotate as much as a quarter of a turn, there is wear in the system. This may well be in the differential. When testing the rear propshaft, make sure that the handbrake is off in order not to get a false impression.

While looking at the transmission, check for wear in the universal joints on the propshaft ends by using a screwdriver as a lever to see if there is appreciable movement between the yoke and the joint. The more movement there is, the more wear there is, too.

Exhaust system ④ ③ ② ①

Begin your checks here by looking at the tailpipe. On V8 models, a light grey deposit inside the pipe is a good sign, but a powdery black deposit suggests the engine is running rich or that the vehicle has been used excessively in low-speed town traffic. Steam from the exhaust of either a petrol or diesel engine suggests head gasket problems (although there may be a small amount on starting a cold engine, caused by condensation in the exhaust pipe). White smoke may point to a leak from the brake servo. On diesel models, the inside of the exhaust pipe is always likely to be a black colour.

On both petrol and diesel models, check the entire system for corrosion, and examine the flexible mountings as well. A stainless steel system is a bonus, as it means you are unlikely ever to need a new exhaust. However, do ask to see evidence, such as an invoice, that the system really is stainless steel.

Several different exhaust systems were fitted over the years, and many V8 models in the 1990s (and late 1980s in North America) had catalytic converters in the exhaust. These 'cats' can be expensive to replace and owners often try to avoid the job, so check whether the vehicle should have a 'cat' system and if so, whether it actually does! If the 'cat' rattles at idle when the engine is warm, it probably needs replacing. Needless to say, a vehicle originally fitted with a catalytic converter exhaust is required to have one to meet roadworthiness regulations in most countries.

Electrical system

Early Range Rovers had a very simple electrical system, but, by the time of the four-doors, customers were demanding more and more extra equipment. That inevitably led to a more complicated system, and from the mid-1980s there was a new thin-wall wiring system with plug connectors instead of the old-fashioned bullet or spade types.

Whatever the age of Range Rover you are looking at, make sure that everything electrical works! Lights are a bare minimum for legal and safety

The high levels of equipment on later models mean that there are more electrical items to check.

reasons, but check the electric windows if fitted, the electric sunroof, the central locking, the electric seat adjustment if fitted, and even the ICE system. (A radio that doesn't work shouldn't put you off buying a vehicle, but it's a bargaining point when you're trying to agree a price with the seller.)

The wiring system on later Range Rovers made it harder for enthusiastic DIY owners to add non-original electrical equipment. However, it all seemed much easier with the simple system of the early models, and owners were more keen to have a go. So it's advisable to have a long and careful look at any wiring that wasn't original to the vehicle. It's not unknown for additional equipment to overload the original wiring and to burn it out – which usually happens suddenly, and on a dark and wet night.

Test drive

You will want to take the vehicle for a test drive before making your mind up whether to buy it. Don't forget that you will need to be insured to drive it, and that not every insurance policy covers you for using somebody else's vehicle. Also worth checking is that the vehicle itself is road legal; if you take a test drive on a public road in a vehicle without a valid roadworthiness certificate, you will be breaking the law.

Engine health and performance

Most people assume the health of the engine is the first thing to check on a test drive. So we'll start with that, but bear in mind that it isn't always the engine that causes the most expensive problems!

The V8 engines should all deliver their power smoothly, although the different versions have different characteristics. The sound of a healthy carburettor engine is very different from that of a late injected 3.9-litre, for example. Listen for undue top-end noise and beware of misfires, which are not always easy to detect in a multi-cylinder engine. A rough and rasping sound from one side of the engine usually means that the exhaust manifold is blowing; it's

This Tdi diesel engine had been allowed to overheat, and the head had cracked in several places between the valve ports. The yellow marks highlight the damage.

unlikely to be cracked, and the remedy is likely to be to tighten the manifold fixings.

The diesel engines are much rougher and much noisier, but they should all pull strongly through the gears. Keep an eye on the temperature gauge when driving a VM diesel engine, because a known weakness is that one of the four separate cylinder head gaskets can blow. Overheating with a diesel of any variety is bad news, so it's best to avoid one with this problem.

After taking any diesel Range Rover for a spirited run, DO NOT switch the engine off as soon as you have come to a halt back at the seller's premises. The turbocharger has been spinning at very high revolutions, and its bearings need to be cooled down by their oil first. So leave the engine idling for a minute or so – longer than absolutely necessary, but a sign of respect for somebody else's property.

Don't expect any Range Rover with a standard engine to be a high-performance machine by modern standards, but if it's very noticeably slow, there's something wrong.

Gearbox assessment

(a) Manual gearbox

You can check how easily the gears go in by depressing the clutch and just trying all positions with the vehicle stationary. However, the real state of the gearbox will be revealed on the move, when baulky synchromesh may prove to be the least of your problems. Noises on the over-run, jumping out of gear, grinding noises from the gearwheels – they all become apparent. Don't forget to try the gearbox in reverse as well.

Note, incidentally, that the early LT77 five-speed gearboxes were notorious for refusing to go into second gear when cold. The cure was to fill them with automatic transmission fluid instead of ordinary gearbox oil, but Land Rover then changed the synchromesh cones in December 1991 to create the LT77S gearbox, which was problem-free in this respect.

On ABS-equipped Range Rovers, the warning light should extinguish when the vehicle reaches 5mph.

The wood trim, if fitted, can be quite easily damaged.

Some body problems are best seen from beneath. This inner front wing has rusted through.

Headlinings often sag, and are best replaced with an aftermarket type, such as this one from Nationwide Trim.

Rusted sills will be hidden behind the plastic sill panels. Feel their inner surfaces for signs of corrosion.

Bull bars at the front were once common, and light guards were also popular. Removing them leaves scars like these.

Alloy wheels can corrode very badly if not regularly cleaned. Refurbishment is possible, but this one may have gone too far.

(b) Automatic gearbox

If the gearbox is a Chrysler three-speed, don't expect quick changes up or down, and don't expect particularly rapid progress, either. However, the good news is that these gearboxes are tough and long-lasting, and don't normally give trouble. Any problems will become apparent during a test run anyway.

Transfer gearbox

The early four-speed (LT95) manual gearbox had an integral two-speed transfer box. All automatics and five-speed models had a separate transfer box, which was gear-driven until mid-1988, when a chain-driven Borg Warner type took over. The chain-driven transfer box was quiet – and if it isn't, there's a problem. The others all suffered from varying degrees of gear whine, and it is really up to you how much you can take. If there are other noises from any type of transfer box, it's best to assume there's a problem.

Always check that the transfer box lever will engage Low range, and that it will select the centre differential lock where applicable. Many Range Rovers spend their entire lives in High ratio, with the result that the Low ratio selector seizes. On the four-speed LT95, the centre differential lock is operated by a separate pull-up switch, and on the Borg Warner transfer box it is automatically operated by a viscous clutch.

Clutch and clutch pedal

Some people find the clutch pedal on manual Range Rovers is heavy, or that its travel is too long. Land Rover made various changes over the years to improve its operation.

Once you're used to the clutch on the example you're testing, a few basic checks will reassure you whether all is well or not. If the clutch squeals when you push the pedal to the floor, the chances are that the release bearing is worn. The parts are not expensive, but fitting can be costly unless you do it yourself, in which case it will take quite a long time. If vehicle speed doesn't increase when you press the accelerator, the clutch is worn and is slipping. Expect the clutch to bite when the pedal is about half-way through its travel; near the top or near the bottom means the adjustment isn't right. Finally, if there's clutch judder as the drive is taken up, you'll need to take a closer look.

Overdrive (if fitted)

Overdrive will only be found on Range Rovers with the four-speed manual gearbox, typically from the later 1970s. It is very definitely a mixed blessing, as it introduces more joints and therefore clunks and bangs into the driveline. Make sure it does engage fully and that it disengages smoothly.

Steering

The steering on a Range Rover was never razor-sharp but it was also never woolly when in good condition. In fact, it is generally well-weighted and well suited to the vehicle. Only very early examples without power assistance can be accused of having heavy steering, and then only at parking speeds. Assess how good the steering is on the one you're testing by seeing if it matches these criteria.

When turning the steering on a stationary vehicle, you are putting a great strain on the power assistance system (which you will only feel in your own muscles on a non-assisted system). So a few groans and creaks in these circumstances should not be a cause for concern. However, if the steering makes any noises on the move at low speeds, it has a problem. Be careful on the rest of your test drive.

Brakes

Range Rover brakes were always power assisted and should pull the vehicle up quickly and in a straight line. On later models with ABS, any loss of traction will be picked up by the ABS system, which will then pump the brakes rapidly and make a chattering noise. This is perfectly normal. The system also makes some curious moaning noises as it cycles and recharges every few minutes, but you won't normally hear those unless the vehicle is stationary with the engine running.

The handbrake operates on the transmission, so do NOT test the handbrake by applying it when the vehicle is moving. If you do, you are likely to cause some expensive damage.

Paperwork
You looked at the paperwork when you did your preliminary assessment. Now's the time to double-check that everything really is in order.

Evaluation procedure
Add up the total points, and see what category the vehicle falls into. The maximum possible score is 144.

125 points = Excellent
95 points = Good
75 points = Average
50 points = Poor

A Range Rover scoring over 80 will be completely usable and will need only regular care and maintenance to preserve its condition. A score between 35 and 70 means some serious work is needed, and this is likely to cost about the same regardless of the actual score. A score lower than 60 means that you are looking at a full restoration.

10 Auctions
– sold! Another way to buy your dream

Auction pros & cons

Pros: Prices will usually be lower than those of dealers or private sellers and you might grab a real bargain on the day. Auctioneers have usually established clear title with the seller. At the venue you can usually examine documentation relating to the vehicle.

Cons: You have to rely on a sketchy catalogue description of condition & history. The opportunity to inspect is limited and you cannot drive the car. Auction cars are often a little below par and may require some work. It's easy to overbid. There will usually be a buyer's premium to pay in addition to the auction hammer price.

Which auction?

Auctions by established auctioneers are advertised in car magazines and on the auction houses' websites. A catalogue, or a simple printed list of the lots for auctions might only be available a day or two ahead, though often lots are listed and pictured on auctioneers' websites much earlier. Contact the auction company to ask if previous auction selling prices are available as this is useful information (details of past sales are often available on websites).

Catalogue, entry fee and payment details

When you purchase the catalogue of the vehicles in the auction, it often acts as a ticket allowing two people to attend the viewing days and the auction. Catalogue details tend to be comparatively brief, but will include information such as 'one owner from new, low mileage, full service history', etc. It will also usually show a guide price to give you some idea of what to expect to pay and will tell you what is charged as a 'Buyer's premium.' The catalogue will also contain details of acceptable forms of payment. At the fall of the hammer an immediate deposit is usually required, the balance payable within 24 hours. If the plan is to pay by cash there may be a cash limit. Some auctions will accept payment by debit card. Sometimes credit or charge cards are acceptable, but will often incur an extra charge. A bank draft or bank transfer will have to be arranged in advance with your own bank as well as with the auction house. No vehicle will be released before *all* payments are cleared. If delays occur in payment transfers then storage costs can accrue.

Buyer's premium

A buyer's premium will be added to the hammer price: *don't* forget this in your calculations. It is not usual for there to be a further state tax or local tax on the purchase price and/or on the buyer's premium.

Viewing

In some instances it's possible to view on the day, or days before, as well as in the hours prior to, the auction. There are auction officials available who are willing to help out by opening engine and luggage compartments and to allow you to inspect the interior. While the officials may start the engine for you, a test drive is out of the question. Crawling under and around the car as much as you want is permitted, but you can't suggest that the car you are interested in be jacked up, or attempt to do the job yourself. You can also ask to see any documentation available.

Bidding

Before you take part in the auction, *decide your maximum bid – and stick to it!*

It may take a while for the auctioneer to reach the lot you are interested in, so use that time to observe how other bidders behave. When it's the turn of your car, attract the auctioneer's attention and make an early bid. The auctioneer will then look to you for a reaction every time another bid is made; usually the bids will be in fixed increments until the bidding slows, when smaller increments will often be accepted before the hammer falls. If you want to withdraw from the bidding, make sure the auctioneer understands your intentions – a vigorous shake of the head when he or she looks to you for the next bid should do the trick!

Assuming that you are the successful bidder, the auctioneer will note your card or paddle number, and from that moment on you will be responsible for the vehicle.

If the vehicle is unsold, either because it failed to reach the reserve or because there was little interest, it may be possible to negotiate with the owner, via the auctioneers, after the sale is over.

Successful bid

There are two more items to think about. How to get the vehicle home, and insurance. If you can't drive the vehicle, your own or a hired trailer is one way; another is to have the vehicle shipped using the facilities of a local company. The auction house will also have details of companies specialising in the transfer of cars.

Insurance for immediate cover can usually be purchased on site, but it may be more cost-effective to make arrangements with your own insurance company in advance, and then call to confirm the full details.

eBay & other online auctions?

eBay & other online auctions could land you a vehicle at a bargain price, though you'd be foolhardy to bid without examining it first, something most vendors encourage. A useful feature of eBay is that the geographical location of the vehicle is shown, so you can narrow your choices to those within a realistic radius of home. Be prepared to be outbid in the last few moments of the auction. Remember, your bid is binding and that it will be very, very difficult to get restitution in the case of a crooked vendor fleecing you – *caveat emptor!*

Be aware that some vehicles offered for sale in online auctions are 'ghost' cars. *Don't* part with *any* cash without being sure that the vehicle does actually exist and is as described (usually pre-bidding inspection is possible).

Auctioneers

Barrett-Jackson – www.barrett-jackson.com
Bonhams – www.bonhams.com
British Car Auctions (BCA) – www.bca-europe.com or www.british-car-auctions.co.uk
Cheffins – www.cheffins.co.uk

Christies – www.christies.com
Coys – www.coys.co.uk
eBay – www.eBay.com or www.eBay.co.uk
H&H – www.classic-auctions.co.uk
RM – www.rmauctions.com
Shannons – www.shannons.com.au
Silver – www.silverauctions.com

11 Paperwork
– correct documentation is essential!

The paper trail
Classic, collector and prestige cars usually come with a large portfolio of paperwork accumulated and passed on by a succession of proud owners. This documentation represents the real history of the car and from it can be deduced the level of care the car has received, how much it's been used, which specialists have worked on it and the dates of major repairs and restorations. All of this information will be priceless to you as the new owner, so be very wary of cars with little paperwork to support their claimed history.

Registration documents
All countries/states have some form of registration for private vehicles whether its like the American 'pink slip' system or the British 'log book' system.

It is essential to check that the registration document is genuine, that it relates to the car in question, and that all the vehicle's details are correctly recorded, including chassis/VIN and engine numbers (if these are shown). If you are buying from the previous owner, his or her name and address will be recorded in the document: this will not be the case if you are buying from a dealer.

In the UK the current (Euro-aligned) registration document is named 'V5C,' and is printed in coloured sections of blue, green and pink. The blue section relates to the car specification, the green section has details of the new owner and the pink section is sent to the DVLA in the UK when the car is sold. A small section in yellow deals with selling the car within the motor trade.

In the UK the DVLA will provide details of earlier keepers of the vehicle upon payment of a small fee, and much can be learned in this way.

If the car has a foreign registration there may be expensive and time-consuming formalities to complete. Do you really want the hassle?

Roadworthiness certificate
Most country/state administrations require that vehicles are regularly tested to prove that they are safe to use on the public highway and do not produce excessive emissions. In the UK that test (the 'MoT') is carried out at approved testing stations, for a fee. In the USA the requirement varies, but most states insist on an emissions test every two years as a minimum, while the police are charged with pulling over unsafe-looking vehicles.

In the UK the test is required on an annual basis once a vehicle becomes three years old. Of particular relevance for older cars is that the certificate issued includes the mileage reading recorded at the test date and, therefore, becomes an independent record of that car's history. Ask the seller if previous certificates are available. Without an MoT the vehicle should be trailered to its new home, unless you insist that a valid MoT is part of the deal. (Not such a bad idea this, as at least you will know the car was roadworthy on the day it was tested and you don't need to wait for the old certificate to expire before having the test done.)

Road licence
The administration of every country/state charges some kind of tax for the use of

its road system, the actual form of the 'road licence' and how it is displayed, varies enormously country to country, and state to state.

Changed legislation in the UK means that the seller of a car must surrender any existing road fund licence, and it is the responsibility of the new owner to re-tax the vehicle at the time of purchase and before the car can be driven on the road. It's therefore vital to see the Vehicle Registration Certificate (V5C) at the time of purchase, and to have access to the New Keeper Supplement (V5C/2), allowing the buyer to obtain road tax immediately.

If the car is untaxed because it has not been used for a period of time, the owner has to inform the licensing authorities, otherwise the vehicle's date-related registration number will be lost, and there will be a painful amount of paperwork to get it re-registered. Also in the UK, vehicles built before the end of 1972 are not subject to an annual road tax payment. Car clubs can often provide formal proof that a particular car qualifies for this valuable concession.

Certificates of authenticity
For many makes of collectible car it is possible to get a certificate proving the age and authenticity (eg engine and chassis numbers, paint colour and trim) of a particular vehicle; these are sometimes called 'Heritage Certificates' and if the car comes with one of these it is a definite bonus. If you want to obtain one, the relevant owners' club is the best starting point.

If the car has been used in European classic car rallies it may have a FIVA (Fédération Internationale des Véhicules Anciens) certificate. The so-called 'FIVA Passport,' or 'FIVA Vehicle Identity Card,' enables organisers and participants to recognise whether or not a particular vehicle is suitable for individual events. If you want to obtain such a certificate go to www.fbhvc. co.uk or www.fiva.org; there will be similar organisations in other countries too.

Valuation certificate
Hopefully, the vendor will have a recent valuation certificate, or letter signed by a recognised expert stating how much he, or she, believes the particular car to be worth (such documents, together with photos, are usually needed to get 'agreed value' insurance). Generally such documents should act only as

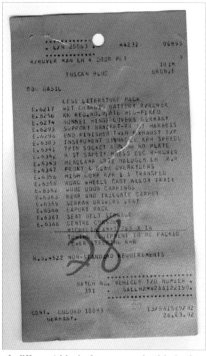

A different kind of paperwork: this is the 'line ticket,' which records the original build specification of a Range Rover. They are sometimes found trapped behind the dashboard or under the headlining. This one dates from 1982.

confirmation of your own assessment of the car rather than a guarantee of value as the expert has probably not seen the car in the flesh. The easiest way to find out how to obtain a formal valuation is to contact the owners' club.

Service history
Often these cars will have been serviced at home by enthusiastic (and hopefully capable) owners for a good number of years. Nevertheless, try to obtain as much service history and other paperwork pertaining to the car as you can. Naturally, dealer stamps, or specialist garage receipts score most points in the value stakes. However, anything helps in the great authenticity game, items like the original bill of sale, handbook, parts invoices and repair bills, adding to the story and the character of the car. Even a brochure correct to the year of the car's manufacture is a useful document and something that you could well have to search hard to locate in future years. If the seller claims that the car has been restored, then expect receipts and other evidence from a specialist restorer.

If the seller claims to have carried out regular servicing, ask what work was completed, when, and seek some evidence of it being carried out. Your assessment of the car's overall condition should tell you whether the seller's claims are genuine.

Restoration photographs
If the seller tells you that the car has been restored, then expect to be shown a series of photographs taken while the restoration was under way. Pictures taken at various stages, and from various angles, should help you gauge the thoroughness of the work. If you buy the car, ask if you can have all the photographs as they form an important part of the vehicle's history. It's surprising how many sellers are happy to part with their car and accept your cash, but want to hang on to their photographs! In the latter event, you may be able to persuade the vendor to get a set of copies made.

12 What's it worth?
– let your head rule your heart

Condition

If the car you've been looking at is really bad, then you've probably not bothered to use the marking system in Chapter 9 – the 60 minute evaluation. You may not have even got as far as using that Chapter at all!

If you did use the marking system in Chapter 9 you'll know whether the car is in Excellent (maybe Concours), Good, Average or Poor condition or, perhaps, somewhere in between these categories.

Many classic/collector car magazines run a regular price guide. If you haven't bought the latest editions, do so now and compare their suggested values for the model you are thinking of buying: also look at the auction prices they're reporting. Range Rover values climbed steeply after about 2010, but some models will always be more sought-after than others. Trends can change too. The values published in the magazines tend to vary from one magazine to another, as do their scales of condition, so read carefully the guidance notes they provide. Bear in mind that a car that is truly a recent show winner could be worth more than the highest scale published. Assuming that the car you have in mind is not in show/concours condition, then relate the level of condition that you judge the car to be in with the appropriate guide price. How does the figure compare with the asking price? Before you start haggling with the seller, consider what affect any variation from standard specification might have on the car's value.

If you are buying from a dealer, remember there will be a dealer's premium on the price.

Desirable options/extras

Many owners consider the most desirable vehicles are the later ones with the injected V8 engines, leather upholstery, air-conditioning, metallic paint, and so on. All these features certainly make it easier to live with a Range Rover. Extras are much more a matter of personal preference. For example, side steps may not improve the appearance of the Range Rover but they may be necessary for some people just to get into the vehicle, which sits quite high off the ground. Similarly, the bodykit available in the 1990s is a matter of taste.

Then again, there are many enthusiasts who think that the plain, unadorned

Range Rovers were often converted for wealthy buyers in the 1970s and 1980s. This is a Glenfrome Ashton convertible, with as much luxury as anyone could want. You won't find one easily, and you'll need deep pockets to keep it up to scratch.

Side steps, sometimes called side runners, are practical for some people.

early two-door models are the best of them all. On those vehicles, the fewer options fitted, the better!

Undesirable features

Generally speaking, non-original features will detract from a vehicle's value – and maybe from its interest as well, if you're looking for a Range Rover that's truly representative of the way they were. So avoid those with engines that were not supplied by the factory, avoid those with non-original paint schemes, and avoid those with non-original interiors. Although a genuine factory option, the early three-speed automatic gearbox is also pretty undesirable.

Whether you want aftermarket accessories that were contemporary with the vehicle is a matter of personal choice. Arguably, they were part of the way it was when new or nearly new. Another argument is that they were not fitted by the factory or one of its dealers, and are therefore not 'original.'

There's an exception to think about. Quite large numbers of Range Rovers were converted and customised by specialist companies in the 1970s and 1980s. Typically, these companies added luxury features, sometimes extending the chassis and modifying the bodywork as well. Most of these conversions were built for the Middle East, and were done by companies such as FLM Panelcraft, Glenfrome, Vantagefield, or Wood & Pickett. These vehicles do turn up from time to time and many enthusiasts find them highly desirable as characteristic of their time. Generally speaking, the quality of the workmanship was superb – better than Land Rover's own!

Striking a deal

Negotiate on the basis of your condition assessment, mileage, and fault rectification cost. Also take into account the car's specification. Be realistic about the value, but don't be completely intractable: a small compromise on the part of the vendor or buyer will often facilitate a deal at little real cost.

13 Do you really want to restore?
– it'll take longer and cost more than you think

First of all, a lot depends on what you mean by restoration. Restoring a neglected Range Rover to everyday running condition is quite different from starting with a vehicle that has been off the road for several years, and trying to return it to the way it was when it left the factory. Never mind the success stories you have heard or read about in magazines: unless you have exceptional skills and determination, plus very deep pockets, you will never make an old Range Rover as good as new. Be realistic about what you want to achieve.

Easiest of all is a rolling restoration, which means that the vehicle remains useable for most of the time and that you improve it in larger or smaller bites as you go along. Hardest of all is what I call a resurrection, where you start with a derelict and create a viable Range Rover from it.

Cost will play a very big part in what you do. It has long been a maxim in the classic car world that any restoration will take twice as long and cost at least twice as much as your original, hard-headed estimate. Having undertaken a major Range Rover restoration – OK, a resurrection – I can agree wholeheartedly with that. And don't run away with the idea that you will be able to sell the completed vehicle for more than you have spent on it. Maybe prices will rise that much in the next 30 years, but not soon enough for you to care.

So if you decide to restore a Range Rover, restore it for yourself. Restore

This partially-restored two-door would be tempting as a restoration project today. When it was pictured in 2001, the serious rot in the windscreen pillar was a major deterrent.

Hidden problems can slow down a restoration. Rot in the top of the bulkhead caused for a radical solution here: the top was cut off a sound bulkhead and welded to the vehicle under restoration.

The lowest point of any restoration looks something like this. Everything has to go back somewhere – and it won't unless you took photographs while you were dismantling.

it to your standards, to your time-scale, and to your budget. Even if you have the skills, the equipment and the premises to do the job, resign yourself to having no free weekends for at least a couple of years. If you don't have all these vital elements and are paying somebody else to do the work, resign yourself to having no money to spend on anything else for a similar period of time: classic car restorers can and do charge handsomely for deploying their skills. And whichever way you decide to go, resign yourself to frustrating

The rebuild progresses, but there's still a long way to go!

waits while vital parts are sourced – or, in a worst case, re-made from scratch.

If all this sounds like a counsel of despair, it really isn't. If you are really committed to getting that Range Rover up and running and looking the way you think it should, the time, the effort and the money will all be worth it in the end. There is nothing quite like the first test drive in your newly-restored Range Rover, even if it does break down after the first 100 yards because you've forgotten to tighten something vital.

Rewiring a Range Rover is not a job for the faint-hearted.

And after that, every little improvement you make will make you feel prouder and prouder. It may well become a lifetime's commitment, but you will probably find that it's worth it. To you, at least.

14 Paint problems
– bad complexion, including dimples, pimples and bubbles

Paint faults generally occur due lack of protection/maintenance, or to poor preparation prior to a respray or touch-up. Some of the following conditions may be present in the car you're looking at:

Orange peel

This appears as an uneven paint surface, similar to the appearance of the skin of an orange. The fault is caused by the failure of atomized paint droplets to flow into each other when they hit the surface. It's sometimes possible to rub out the effect with proprietary paint cutting/rubbing compound or very fine grades of abrasive paper. A respray may be necessary in severe cases. Consult a bodywork repairer/paint shop for advice on the particular car.

Cracking

Severe cases are likely to have been caused by too heavy an application of paint (or filler beneath the paint). Also, insufficient stirring of the paint before application can lead to the components being improperly mixed, and cracking can result. Incompatibility with the paint already on the panel can have a similar effect. To rectify the problem it is necessary to rub down to a smooth, sound finish before respraying the problem area.

Crazing

Sometimes the paint takes on a crazed rather than a cracked appearance when the problems mentioned under 'Cracking' are present. This problem can also be caused by a reaction between the underlying surface and the paint. Paint removal and respraying the problem area is usually the only solution.

Blistering

Almost always caused by corrosion of the metal beneath the paint. Usually perforation will be found in the metal and the damage will usually be worse than that suggested by the area of blistering. The metal will have to be repaired before repainting.

Micro blistering

Usually the result of an economy respray where inadequate heating has allowed moisture to settle on the car before spraying. Consult a paint specialist, but usually damaged paint will have to be removed before partial or full respraying. Can also be caused by car covers that don't 'breathe.'

Fading

Some colours, especially reds, are prone to fading if subjected to strong sunlight for long periods without the benefit of polish protection. Sometimes proprietary paint restorers and/or paint cutting/rubbing compounds will retrieve the situation. Often a respray is the only real solution.

Peeling

Often a problem with metallic paintwork when the sealing lacquer becomes damaged and begins to peel off. Poorly applied paint may also peel. The remedy is to strip and start again!

Dimples

Dimples in the paintwork are caused by the residue of polish (particularly silicone types) not being removed properly before respraying. Paint removal and repainting is the only solution.

Dents

Small dents are usually easily cured by the 'Dentmaster,' or equivalent process, that sucks or pushes out the dent (as long as the paint surface is still intact). Companies offering dent removal services usually come to your home: consult your telephone directory.

15 Problems due to lack of use

– just like their owners, Range Rovers need exercise!

Cars, like humans, are at their most efficient if they exercise regularly. A run of at least ten miles, once a week, is recommended for classics.

Seized components
Pistons in calipers, slave and master cylinders can seize. The clutch may seize if the plate becomes stuck to the flywheel because of corrosion. Handbrakes (parking brakes) can seize if the cables and linkages rust. Pistons can seize in the bores due to corrosion.

Fluids
Old, acidic oil can corrode bearings. Uninhibited coolant can corrode internal waterways – a particular problem with the V8 engine, which has aluminium heads and block. Lack of antifreeze can cause core plugs to be pushed out, even cracks in the block or head. Silt settling and solidifying can cause overheating.

Brake fluid absorbs water from the atmosphere and should be renewed every two years. Old fluid with a high water content can cause corrosion and pistons/calipers to seize (freeze), and can cause brake failure when the water turns to vapour near hot braking components.

Range Rovers do not take kindly to being unused for long periods. It's best to check everything systematically and carefully when recommissioning one.

Tyre problems
Tyres that have had the weight of the car on them in a single position for some time will develop flat spots, resulting in some (usually temporary) vibration. The tyre walls may have cracks or (blister-type) bulges, meaning new tyres are needed.

Shock absorbers (dampers)
With lack of use, the dampers will lose their elasticity or even seize. Creaking, groaning and stiff suspension are signs of this problem.

Rubber and plastic
Radiator hoses may have perished and split, possibly resulting in the loss of all coolant. Window and door seals can harden and leak. Gaiters/boots can crack. Wiper blades will harden.

Electrics
The battery will be of little use if it has not been charged for many months. Earthing/grounding problems are common when the connections have corroded. Old bullet and spade type electrical connectors (mostly found on earlier Range Rovers) commonly rust/corrode and will need disconnecting, cleaning and protection (eg Vaseline). Sparkplug electrodes will often have corroded in an unused engine. Wiring insulation can harden and fail.

Rotting exhaust system
Exhaust gas contains a high water content so exhaust systems corrode very quickly from the inside when the vehicle is not used.

16 The Community
– key people, organisations and companies in the Range Rover world

Like Land Rovers, Range Rovers have an enthusiast following that is pretty much worldwide. There is unfortunately not space here to cover the key members of the Range Rover community in every country, so these listings are confined to the UK – and, even then, are far from exhaustive. For details of clubs, specialists and suppliers in other countries, please consult a 4x4 or Land Rover magazine, or check on the internet.

Clubs
There are many local and regional Land Rover clubs in the UK that welcome Range Rovers. However, you may find that the emphasis of your local club is more on off-road driving (typically greenlaning) or on competitive motorsport (typically trialling) than on meticulous restoration for what US enthusiasts call 'show'n'shine' events. Many clubs of course cater for all forms of the hobby.

There is one club that is dedicated to Range Rovers, and covers Range Rovers of all types (not just the first generation models). This is the Range Rover Register, which can be found on the web at www.rrr.co.uk and can be contacted by telephone on 01908 667901.

The Range Rover Register was established in 1985, when the first-generation models were still in production.

Main spares suppliers
John Craddock Ltd, North Street, Bridgtown, Cannock, Staffordshire WS11 0AZ. 01543 577207, or www.johncraddockltd.co.uk

Dunsfold DLR, Alfold Road, Dunsfold, Surrey GU8 4NP. 01483 200567, www. dunsfold.com or dlr@dunsfold.com

Paddock Spares and Accessories, The Showground, The Cliff, Matlock, Derbyshire DE4 5EW. 01629 760877, www.paddockspares.com or sales@paddockspares.com

Rimmer Brothers, Triumph House, Sleaford Road, Bracebridge Heath, Lincoln LN4 2NA. 01522 568000, www.rimmerbros.co.uk or LRsales@rimmerbros.co.uk

Specialist restorers

Kingsley Cars Ltd, A40 Eynsham Bypass, Eynsham. Witney OX29 4EF. 01865 884488, www.kingsleycars.co.uk or sales@kingsleycars.co.uk

Range Rover Reborn, c/o Land Rover Classic. www.landrover.co.uk

Twenty-Ten Engineering, 101 Bartleet Road, Redditch, Worcestershire B98 0DQ. 07973 831878, or enquiries@twentytenengineering.co.uk

Vehicle information

If you are keen to find out about the history of your own vehicle, start with the archives section of the British Motor Museum at Gaydon (01926 641188). They can normally tell you when your Range Rover left the assembly lines, when it left the factory en route for a Land Rover dealer, and who that dealer was. Their records will also reveal what colour it was originally. For a fee, they will provide you with a certificate that contains the available details and is a worthwhile addition to any enthusiast's vehicle paperwork.

However, if your Range Rover was built from CKD – shipped overseas as a kit of parts for assembly outside the UK – or if it went to a specialist converter, less information will be available from this source.

Magazines

Classic Land Rover, Key Publishing Ltd, PO Box 100, Stamford PE9 1XQ. 01780 755131 or www.classiclandrover.com

Land Rover Monthly, The Publishing House, 2 Brickfields Business Park, Woolpit, Suffolk IP30 9QS. www.lrm.co.uk

Land Rover Owner International, Bauer, Media House, Lynchwood, Peterborough PE2 6EA. www.lro.com

Books

How to modify Land Rover Discovery, Defender & Range Rover, by Ralph Hosier, Veloce Publishing, ISBN 978-1-845843-15-1

Original Range Rover: The Restorer's Guide to All Carburettor Models 1970-1986, by James Taylor, Herridge & Sons Ltd, ISBN 978-1-906133-55-9

Range Rover Gold Portfolio 1970-1985 (Brooklands Books Road Test Series) by RM Clarke, Brooklands Books Ltd, ISBN 1-85520-314-6

Range Rover Gold Portfolio 1985-1995 (Brooklands Books Road Test Series) by RM Clarke, Brooklands Books Ltd, ISBN 1-85520-320-0

Range Rover. The First Fifty, by Roger Crathorne, Geof Miller, Gary Pusey and James Taylor, Brooklands Books Ltd, ISBN 978-1-78318-002-8

Range Rover. The First Generation, by James Taylor and Nick Dimbleby, The Crowood Press Ltd, ISBN 1-86126-554-9

17 Vital statistics
– essential data at your fingertips

Production history

It helps to understand what you're looking at if you have some idea of how the Range Rover evolved during nearly 26 years in production. So, here's a breakdown of the key changes; there were very many more minor ones.

1970	Two-door model introduced; V8 only; PVC upholstery.
1973	Brushed nylon upholstery available, optional at first.
1981	Four-door model joins two-door; fabric upholstery standard.
1982	Automatic gearbox becomes optional.
1984	Injected V8 becomes available, initially on Vogue models only.
1985	ZF four-speed automatic replaces Chrysler three-speed.
1986	First diesel option: 2.4-litre made by VM, manual gearbox only.
1988	First Range Rovers with leather and wood interiors (Vogue SE).
1989	V8 engine goes to 3.9 litres (this happened in 1988 for the US market); VM diesel goes to 2.5 litres.
1992	Air suspension replaces coil springs on top models; long-wheelbase model added to range as Vogue LSE (called County LWB in USA); 200Tdi diesel engine replaced VM type.
1994	Completely revised dashboard with airbags for driver and passenger (March). Long-wheelbase models discontinued and standard-wheelbase renamed and badged Range Rover Classic. More refined 300Tdi diesel engine.
1996	Last of the first generation Range Rovers built.

Chassis numbers

Between 1970 and 1979, vehicles had a chassis number with a distinctive three-figure prefix. From mid-1979 (ie the start of the 1980 model-year), vehicles used the international standard of the VIN (Vehicle Identification Number) system, which has a longer alphanumeric prefix to identify type and specification.

1970-1979

Chassis numbers consist of three units. The first one indicates the type, the next is a serial number, and the final letter indicates design changes thought to be significant for dealers servicing the vehicles.

The type codes are 355 (home market), 356 (RHD export, 357 (RHD, CKD), 358 (LHD) and 359 (LHD, CKD). The final letters run from A to G.

1980-1996

From October 1, 1979, chassis numbers conformed to internationally-agreed VIN (Vehicle Identification Number) code standards. VINs used for the first year (ie 1980 model-year) had 14 characters. From November 1, 1980, three further characters (SAL) were added to the prefix, making 17 characters in all. A breakdown of the prefix codes is shown on the following page.

There were various different types of chassis plate over the years, as ownership of the Land Rover marque changed. This one carries the VIN prefix SALLHBM33KA; you can work out from the table below what model it is and when it was built.

SAL	Manufacturer code (from 1 November 1980)
LH	Range Rover
A	100-inch wheelbase
	B = 108-inch wheelbase (ie LSE)
B	Two-door body
	A = Two-door 'van' body
	M = Four-door body
	R = Monteverdi four-door conversion
V	3.5-litre V8 carburettor petrol engine
	E = 2.4-litre VM diesel engine
	F = 2.5-litre 200Tdi or 300 Tdi diesel engine
	L = 3.5-litre V8 injected petrol engine
	M = 3.9-litre V8 injected petrol engine
	N = 2.5-litre VM diesel engine
	3 = 4.2-litre V8 petrol engine
1	RHD with 4-speed manual gearbox
	2 = LHD with 4-speed manual gearbox
	3 = RHD, automatic
	4 = LHD, automatic
	7 = RHD with 5-speed manual gearbox
	8 = LHD with 5-speed manual gearbox
A	Model code (all Range Rovers to mid-1984)

	B = 1985 model-year	H = 1991 model-year
	C = 1986 model-year	J = 1992 model-year
	D = 1987 model-year	K = 1993 model-year
	E = 1988 model-year	L = 1994 model-year
	F = 1989 model-year	M = 1995 model-year
	G = 1990 model-year	

A	Assembled at Solihull
	F = Shipped as KD (knock down) for overseas assembly
123456	Serial number

Note that US models had a different system for the model-year identifier, as follows:

H = 1987 model-year   N = 1992 model-year
J = 1988 model-year   P = 1993 model-year
K = 1989 model-year   R = 1994 model-year
L = 1990 model-year   S = 1995 model-year
M= 1991 model-year

Although Range Rover production continued beyond the normal end of the 1995 model-year, all those built up to January 1996 were considered to be 1995 models and were numbered as such.

This badge was only used on Range Rovers in the 1970s, but the parentage was always the same.

The Essential Buyer's Guide™ series ...

... don't buy a vehicle until you've read one of these!

ALSO FROM VELOCE:

ISBN: 978-1-845850-14-2
Paperback • 19.5x13.9cm
64 pages • 106 colour pictures

ISBN: 978-1-845844-42-4
Paperback • 19.5x13.9cm
64 pages • 113 colour pictures

Having an *Essential Buyer's Guide* in your pocket is just like having a real marque expert by your side. Benefit from the author's years of ownership, learn how to spot a bad vehicle quickly, and how to assess a promising one like a professional. Get the right car at the right price!

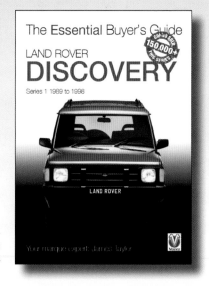

ISBN: 978-1-787112-41-4
Paperback • 19.5x13.9cm
64 pages • 95 pictures

MORE FROM JAMES TAYLOR:

Land Rover's coil-sprung models include the first-generation Range Rover, One Ten family, Defender family and first-generation Discovery models. All have been taken into service by the British armed forces, and this unique book describes and illustrates their uses and adaptations, while containing comprehensive vehicle lists and contract details.

ISBN: 978-1-787112-40-7
Hardback • 25x25cm
144 pages • 275 pictures

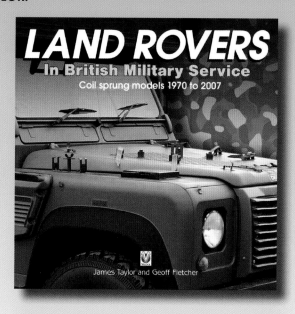

This book tells the story of the use of Land Rovers by the emergency services over a period of nearly 70 years. Examples of the major conversions for Fire, Police and Ambulance use are featured, showing how the different types have been adapted for these specialist roles.

ISBN: 978-1-787112-44-5
Hardback • 25x25cm
144 pages • 275 pictures

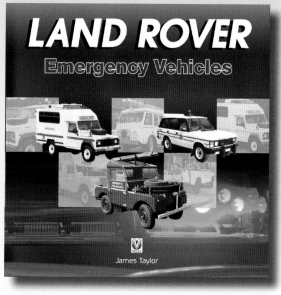

For more information and price details, visit our website at www.veloce.co.uk
email: info@veloce.co.uk • Tel: +44(0)1305 260068

Index